A New True Book

FOREST FIRES

By Arlene Erlbach

Special thanks to Marion Witdmann, Bill Wrenn,
and the USDA Forest Service

Children's Press®
A Division of Grolier Publishing
New York   London   Hong Kong   Sycrey
Danbury, Connecticut

This sign warns motorists not to throw out lit matches or cigarettes.

This book is dedicated to Fran Dyra, a "peach of an editor."

Library of Congress Cataloging-in-Publication Data

Erlbach, Arlene.
  Forest fires / by Arlene Erlbach.
    p. cm. — (A New true book)
    ISBN 0-516-01085-9
    1. Forest fires — Juvenile literature. 2. Forest
fires — United States — Juvenile literature. [1.
Forest fires. 2. Fire ecology. 3. Ecology.] I. Title.
SD421.23.E75 1995   95-12933
634.9'618—dc20   CIP
                                          AC

PHOTO CREDITS

AP/Wide World Photos—27

H. Armstrong Roberts—© E. Degginger, 12 (left); © M. Schneiders, 21 (bottom); © A. Wycheck/Camerique, 32, 40

Photri—4 (top right), 9, 23 (right), 39; © C.W. Biedel, M.D., 23 (left); © Susan Gail Arey, 29 (right); © Les Riess, 33 (left)

© Porterfield/Chickering—2

Root Resources—© MacDonald Photog., 33 (right); © Ted Farrington, 43

Reuters/Bettmann—38

Tom Stack & Associates—© Wendy Shattil/Bob Rozinski, 12 (right), 35 (left); © Dianna L. Stratton, 18; © Inca Spence, 31

Tony Stone Images—© Chris Johns, cover, 25 (right), 37; © Glen Allison, 4 (bottom); Brett Baunton, 6, 45; © Charles A Mauzy, 16; © Tom Ulrich, 21 (top); © Chip Henderson, 29 (left);

UPI/Bettmann Newsphotos—10

Valan—© Phillip Norton, 25 (left); © Tom W. Parkin, 35 (right), 41

Visuals Unlimited—© LINK, 4 (top left); © Herb Greene 7; © Bill Beatty, (14 left); © Mark S. Skalny, 14 (bottom right); © Doug Sokell, 14 (top right);

Cover—Fire fighter silhouetted by burning forest

CONTENTS

FORESTS AND FIRE

Forests are one of our most important natural resources. They provide cool, beautiful places for people to picnic and camp.

Wood, used to make furniture, paper, and houses, comes from forests. Many kinds of plants and animals live there. Forests soak up large amounts of rainfall. This prevents the

5

rapid runoff of water that
often causes flooding.
Forests also provide
drinking water for about
one half the population of
the United States.

Because forests are so important, forest fires are dangerous. They can damage valuable acres of timber and destroy homes. People and animals can be injured or killed. As more people move into or near forests, this type of disaster becomes common.

A dangerous fire in southern California

7

WHAT MAKES FIRE?

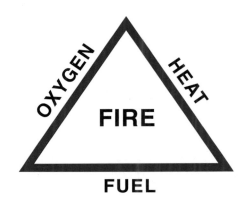

To understand why forest fires occur, we need to know what fire is. Fire is heat and light being given off when something burns. It occurs when oxygen, or air, and fuel are heated to a high temperature.

Before a fire can start, three conditions must be present. There must be fuel that will burn. The fuel must be heated to a high temperature, and there must be plenty of oxygen. Once fire begins, if one of these substances is taken away, the fire dies.

Firefighters try to remove oxygen from a fire by smothering it with dirt.

We call substances that fuel fire *flammable* or *inflammable*. Both words have the same meaning.

Wood, paper, dried leaves, and grass are flammable. If sparks or flames come in contact with these materials, a fire is likely to begin.

Firefighters water down the dry forest floor to stop a fire from spreading.

HOW DOES LIGHTNING CAUSE FOREST FIRES?

Lightning causes more than ten thousand U.S. forest fires annually. That is about ten percent of all forest fires each year. But not all lightning strikes cause forest fires. Lightning must be hot stroke lightning because it lasts longer and creates more heat.

As it strikes a tree, hot stroke lightning splinters it into many pieces. Often a fire starts within the standing tree trunk, or in the ground debris.

HOW DO HUMANS CAUSE FOREST FIRES?

Each year, in the United States, more than ninety thousand forest fires occur because of human carelessness. Maybe somebody drops a lit cigarette, or a family does not completely douse its campfire. Just a few leftover sparks can start a forest fire.

13

An empty jar or bottle
carelessly left on the ground
can cause a fire, too. The
glass focuses the sun's heat
just like a magnifying glass
does. The heat may cause a
dry leaf to burn. Then a
forest fire can occur.

HOW CAN FOREST FIRES HELP A FOREST?

Most forest fires are harmful. Under certain conditions, however, some forest fires are helpful. Carefully controlled fires burn away the dried leaves, branches, and pine needles covering the forest floor. Clearing away the debris helps renew plant growth.

15

New growth in a forest after a fire

It enables sun and water to reach new sprouts, which in turn become food for animals. It also eliminates a fuel source for future fires.

Ashes from the fire put important nutrients back into the soil. When it rains, minerals from the ashes seep into the ground. Plants absorb the nutrients through their roots.

Certain trees—like the lodgepole pine—actually reproduce during a fire. Lodgepole pines produce cones that contain seeds.

A sticky substance called resin seals the cones. Fire melts the resin and opens the cones. The cones then

As wind and animals carry new seeds into the forest, they take root in the ground. Soon they sprout leaves and flowers. One such plant, with magenta flowers, grows rapidly after a forest fire. It is called fireweed.

Sometimes the growth of new plants brings new species of animals to the forest.

Above: Fireweed
after a fire.
Right: A burned
tree sprouts new
life.

WHAT HAPPENS TO ANIMALS DURING A FOREST FIRE?

Large, uncontrolled forest fires kill insects, young birds, and mammals each year. Fish can die, too, when fire changes the condition of the water.

To escape fire, some animals run or fly to a place they think will be safe. Some stay inside their

Forest fires can destroy vital food and water sources of animals.

underground burrows.
Others try diving into lakes
or ponds, although they
cannot stay there for long.
If a fire gets out of hand,
nothing and no one is safe.

KINDS OF FOREST FIRES

Most forest fires are surface fires. They burn debris, like fallen leaves, twigs, and other decaying matter on the forest floor.

If a surface fire spreads to the treetops, then it becomes a crown fire. Crown fires travel from treetop to treetop.

If left unchecked, a surface fire (left) will develop into a crown fire (below).

Sometimes a forest fire goes beneath the soil and burns below the surface. This is a ground fire. It can last for days or weeks if it has enough fuel.

In some cases, a ground fire may seem to vanish, but it is actually burning slowly under the surface. If it continues to be fed, it can become a subsurface fire. Then it may last for weeks or even months.

If fed by a coal seam, the
fire could travel for miles.
Eventually, it could even
appear above ground, far
from where it started.

DETECTING FOREST FIRES

Foresters protect and manage our parks and forests. They are in charge of many workers.

Some workers, called fireguards, watch for forest fires from lookout towers high above ground. Others patrol the forests in small aircraft. At the first

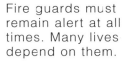

Fire guards must remain alert at all times. Many lives depend on them.

sign of fire, they radio the central office where the fire dispatcher, or fire control officer, decides how to deal with the fire.

29

MAKING DECISIONS ABOUT FOREST FIRES

One of a forester's most important jobs is to determine how to handle a forest fire. He or she must decide when to extinguish a forest fire, or if it should be done at all.

Many parks and forests have "natural burn policies." This means that foresters may allow small

Water is used to keep controlled burns in check.

lightning-caused fires to
burn under certain
conditions. Wind, moisture,
heat, and fuel all have to
be right before foresters
allow a fire to burn.

Firefighters carefully watch the movement of the fire and the wind.

Foresters believe some fires are part of the natural process of forest life, and that it is healthy for a forest to be cleared of debris that may fuel larger forest fires. However, foresters watch these fires carefully so that the fires do not get out of hand.

Weather helps foresters decide how to handle forest fires. For example, if a forest fire occurs on a dry, windy day, it can spread quickly.

Signs like these are placed throughout parks to remind visitors of fire safety.

Then foresters may decide to stop the fire. Foresters usually let a fire burn if the air is damp. In damp air, a fire will often burn itself out. If rain or snow is predicted, foresters often wait to let nature douse the fire.

In 1988, uncontrolled fires burned in Yellowstone National Park all summer. Almost ten thousand firefighters could not put out the fires. Finally, in October, rain and snow drowned the fires.

Left: The results of the 1988 fire in Yellowstone National Park.
Right: Foresters use a drip torch to ignite a controlled fire to
burn debris.

Sometimes foresters set
fires deliberately. These are
called prescribed burns.
Prescribed burns clear
away debris that could fuel
a larger fire.

FIGHTING FOREST FIRES

To fight forest fires, firefighters eliminate one of the three necessary conditions of fire: fuel, oxygen, and heat. They battle the blaze on the ground and from planes in the air.

Firefighters may cut down strips of trees to stop a fire.

Firefighters dig a trench to stop an approaching fire.

They use bulldozers, axes, and saws. The area of cut trees is called a fire line.

After making a fire line, firefighters might set backfires to burn the area

Firefighters set a
backfire to stop the
spread of fire in
Malibu, California.

between the fire line and the
forest fire. When the forest
fire reaches the fire line, the
fire stops. It has no fuel to
feed it.

If a fire is small, local
crews of firefighters will battle
it. If a fire gets out of hand,
firefighters may be called in
from many locations.

In fire areas that are difficult to get at, special crews called smoke jumpers parachute down from planes.

While crews fight the fire on the ground, other firefighters work from the air. From planes, they drop fire retardant over the foliage ahead of the fire.

Plane releasing fire retardant over fire area

The fire retardant is a chemical that looks like watery, red gelatin. It makes the foliage too wet to burn.

Some forest fires break out near lakes or rivers. To stop these fires, helicopter pilots collect water in huge buckets and pour it over the foliage ahead of the fire to prevent it from burning. They also drop water along the sides and rear of the fire to smother it.

Helicopter dumping water on the fire area

SMOKEY BEAR

More than ninety years ago, the U.S. Forest Service began encouraging people to prevent forest fires. In the 1940s, posters about fire prevention featured Bambi, a Walt Disney character. It became the United States fire-prevention symbol.

Then, in 1944, the Forest Service chose a bear as its fire-prevention symbol. The bear was named Smokey.

YOU CAN HELP THE FOREST, TOO

It is important that everyone take part in preventing forest fires. Here are some rules for being careful when you picnic or camp.

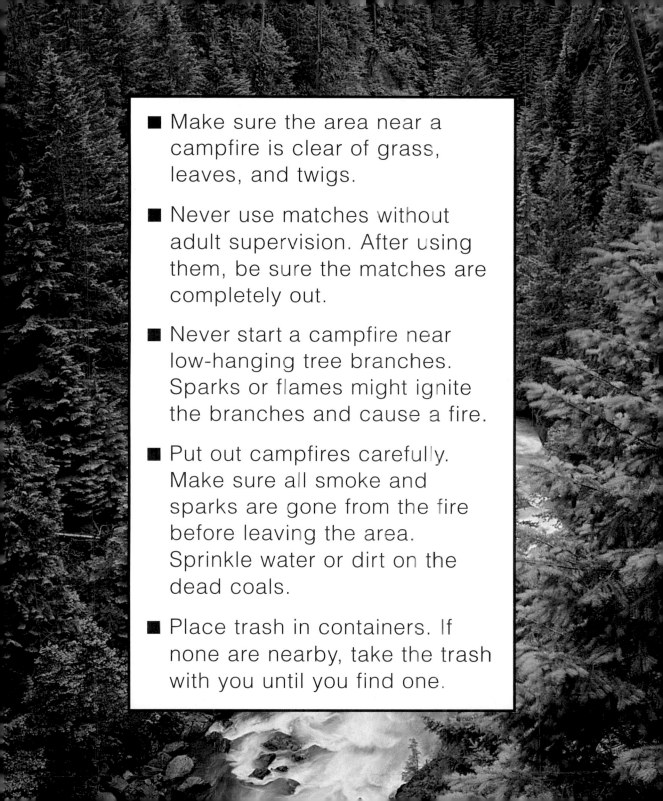

- Make sure the area near a campfire is clear of grass, leaves, and twigs.

- Never use matches without adult supervision. After using them, be sure the matches are completely out.

- Never start a campfire near low-hanging tree branches. Sparks or flames might ignite the branches and cause a fire.

- Put out campfires carefully. Make sure all smoke and sparks are gone from the fire before leaving the area. Sprinkle water or dirt on the dead coals.

- Place trash in containers. If none are nearby, take the trash with you until you find one.

GLOSSARY

acre (ā´ker) — an area of land equal to 4,840 square yards

backfire (băk fīr) — a fire that is started to clear an area in order to stop an advancing fire

bulldozer (boŏl´dō zer) — a big tractor with a huge metal shovel in front for moving things

burrow (bur´ō) — a hole dug in the ground by a small animal

coal seam (kōl sēm) — an underground area of coal thick enough to mine

cone (kōn) — a group of woody, overlapping scales containing the seeds of an evergreen tree

crew (kroŏ) — a group of people who work together

crown fire (kroun fīr) — a fire that has spread to the treetops

debris (dĕ brē´) — the remains of fallen leaves and branches on the forest floor

disaster (dĭ zăs´ter) — something that causes destruction and death

dispatcher (di spăch´er) — person who sends a message

douse (dous) — to wet completely with water; drench

fuel (fyoo´el) — a substance that is burned to give off heat or produce energy, such as coal, wood, gas, or oil

firefighter (fīr´fīt´er) — a person whose job is to put out fires

fireguard (fīr´gärd) — a person whose job is to watch for fires

fire line (fīr līn) — an area that has been cleared of trees and debris to prevent the spread of an advancing fire

fireweed (fīrwēd) — pinkish purple flowers that grow after a fire

flammable (flăm´e bel) — something that burns easily

46

foliage (fō′lē ĭj) — leaves of plants and trees

forester (for′ĭster) — a person who works in developing and caring for forests

ground fire — a fire that burns below the surface of the soil

inflammable (ĭn flăm′e bel) — something that catches fire easily

lightning (līt′nĭng) — a flash of light in the sky caused by electricity passing between clouds or between a cloud and the ground

natural burn policy — a decision made by foresters to allow a fire, that was started by lightning, to burn under careful supervision

natural resource (năch′er el rē′sors) — something in nature that is necessary to people

nutrient (noo′trē ent) — something that nourishes, such as an ingredient in food

oxygen (ŏk′sĭ jen) — a gaseous chemical element necessary for the start of a fire; also needed for plants and animals to live

prescribed burn (prĕ skrībd′ bern) — fires that foresters set deliberately and control

prevent (prē vent′) — to stop

resin (rĕz′ĭn) a yellowish brown substance that oozes from some trees and plants and is used in making varnish and plastic

retardant (rē′tar dent) — something that holds back or slows down something else

runoff — water that enters streams and lakes from ground that has soaked up rain

smother (smŭth′er) — to put out a fire by removing the oxygen supply

substance (sŭb′stens) — what a thing is made of

subsurface fire (sŭb′sŭr fes fīr) — a fire, which is fueled by coal or another fuel below the surface of the ground

surface fire (sur′fes fīr) — a fire, which burns debris on the forest floor

timber (tĭm′ber) — trees, or land covered with trees; wood for building

weather (wĕth′er) — the condition of the air

INDEX

ABOUT THE AUTHOR

Arlene Erlbach has written thirty books for young people in many genres including fiction and nonfiction.
She has a master's degree in special education. In addition to being an author of children's books, she is a learning disabilities teacher at Gray School in Chicago, Illinois. Arlene loves to encourage children to write and is in charge of her school's Young Authors program.